This book is a gift to

Super Kid _____

from _____

For permissions and quantity sales email:
info@ThisLittleLightProductions.com

Related apparel and accessories
can be found in our online store:
www.SuperKidClub.com
Every purchase goes towards helping
children in need around the world.

Nose-blowing 101 for super kids

By Suzy Vreeland

Illustrator Maruf Hasan

This Little Light
PRODUCTIONS
www.thislittlelightproductions.com

*Thanks to Allison, Brandon and Carla for your roles in the story!
Thanks also to Genkiworld for your great insight and input,
to Maruf for being the best illustrator, to Grace for your tip,
to brusheezy.com for their brush choices and to Carla too
for your support and understanding in all of this!*

*Children light up the world.
May we do what we can to help their light shine brightly.
Thank you to my daughter for lighting up my world.*

Book Note

Part 1 - The Challenge
Part 2 - The Solution

Let me catch it,
Let me catch it,
Let me get that lil nose of yours.

I've got a tissue
Quick quick, quick.

Yes, there it is.

Oh no, I let it go.

Here nearly ...

Oh quick, I got it!

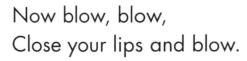

Now blow, blow,
Close your lips and blow.

...Uh oh!
Come on, pleease,
Let me get those shnoozzies out.

Pleeease.

There, I got it,

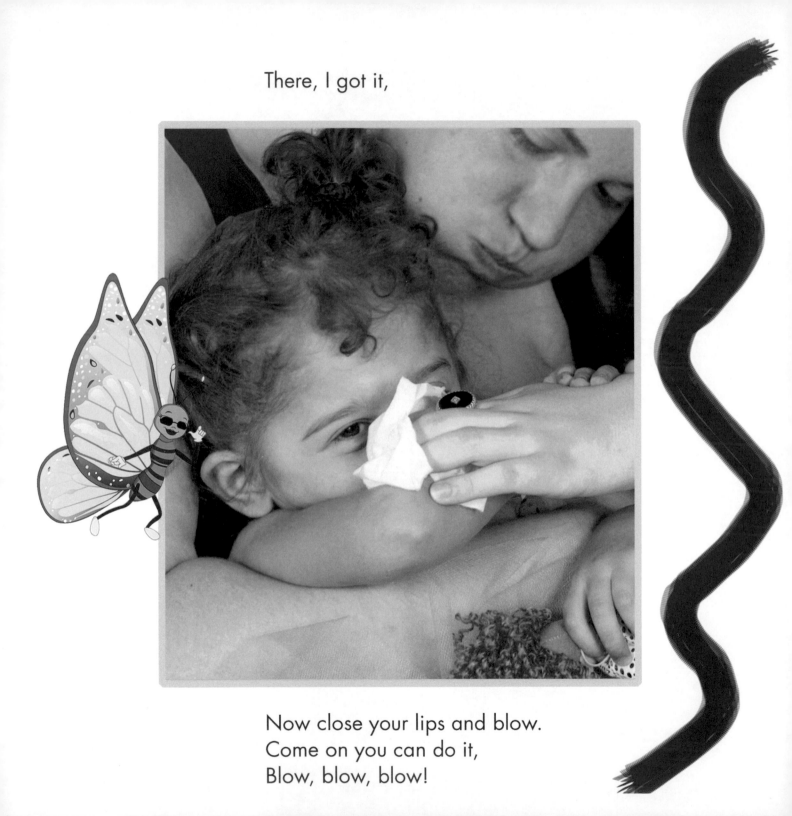

Now close your lips and blow.
Come on you can do it,
Blow, blow, blow!

Come on, let me catch that lil nose again.

You'll feel better,
You will see.

Let me catch it.. here, look at me.

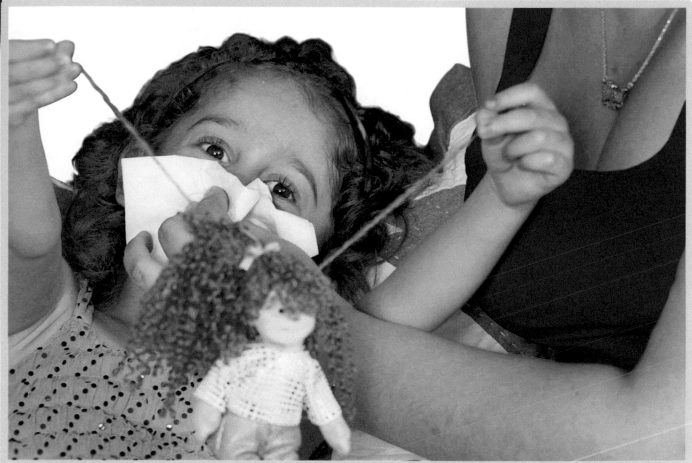

Blow again, That's it, **YiPPeee** !!!!

Now your nose is clear!
You did it, you did it, you did it!
Yippeeeeeeee !!!!

END Part 1

Now we've reached the end of Part 1.
Turn the page to continue to Part 2 whenever ready..

Parents & Caregivers, this can be saved
for a while until your child has
gotten just a little older.. ;)

Or if you choose, it's okay to continue now.

PART 2
begins next

(only if your child has been trying...)

Now that you're becoming such
big girls and boys you know ...

That clearing your nose is the way to go.

Because Fairy Princesses and Super Heroes
get colds too.. even they need to learn what to do!

Swinging 'tween buildings,
keeping an eye on the town.

Or seeking out fairies,
while exploring all around.

These things you can't do if you're all stuffed up,

Sneezing and sniffing ... froggies in your throat ...
Aaachoo!! .... Rrribbit, rrrribbit!
Eyes are all watery ... chest is clogged
Cough!.. Cough!!

To help you get better, and feeling anew,
here is what you need to do:

Take a big breath,
let me see you do it.

Close your lips ...
like this mmmm,
...like a bumblebee.

Now tighten your tummy
it does feel funny,

 And pussshh the air
through !

Now we squeeze then wipe
and do it all over again..

(..don't forget to wash your hands..)

It's very good practice for being ladies and men.

Or should we say, Princesses and Super Friends.

Then you'll feel clearer and
be able to breathe.

Remember, "If at first you don't succeed [fill in the blanks]

try, t _____, t _____ a_____n ! "

And " practice makes **p_____t ! "**

Now if you eat good, healthy food and rest,

You'll be back on track soon and feeling your best!

Make the Dove Fly game

Another good exercise to assist in mastering this skill is the "make the dove fly", game.

• Hold a tissue/hankie on your index finger and slowly move it up and down close to your child's face.

• Tell your child that you are going to play a game of pretend where the tissue/hankie is a dove, and you want to make it fly by blowing on it with just the nose.

• Close off one of their nostrils, while asking them to see how much they can make the dove fly, while you move it slightly further away each time.

• With each blow encourage them to see if they can make the dove fly higher by blowing harder, alternating nostrils for practice.

May our children continue to play outside as much as possible, and explore both nature and their creativity.

50931450R00020

Made in the USA
Columbia, SC
12 February 2019